"Dr. Hollman has developed a concept that gives parents a method to help themselves and their children to cope with the emotional challenges of childhood and adolescence. Using her method of 'Parental Intelligence,' parents are guided through the steps leading to the relief of anxiety and ultimately to a closer bond between parent and child.

Using clear language and numerous examples, Dr. Hollman opens up the world of compassionate and empathic relationships to all of us.

Dr. Hollman has transformed her many years of clinical experience and study into an immensely useful guide for parents and clinicians to help children and parents develop stronger familial relationships and relieve the stress and anxiety that may develop at different stages of childhood.

Parenthetically, these methods work just as effectively for all relationships.

This is a book that should be read by all parents and clinicians. Thank you, Dr. Hollman."

—ERNEST KOVACS, MD, FAPA, DIPLOMATE

American Board Psychiatry and Neurology; Clinical Professor of Albert Einstein College of Medicine; Supervisor in Family and Marital Therapy, Zucker Hillside Psychiatric Residence Program

"Anxiety is both a ubiquitous and worrisome group of emotions that all children and adolescents and their parents need to negotiate throughout the lifespan. Dr. Hollman takes the reader through a series of experiences with low-grade to severe anxieties associated with child and adolescent development. Each type of anxiety is described, with illustrations of the grip anxiety can have in the short or long term, depending on how soon interventions are available to reduce its effects.

The approach is masterful in that Dr. Hollman describes how parents can be thorough enough in locating the surrounding elements behind a state of anxiety while empathizing and accepting the symptoms. This combination of being a psychological detective and a supportive adult work well together. Often the past is converging with the present situation, and parents are advised to take stock of where they are in the situation. Were [the child's] anxieties attended to in helpful ways, did the anxiousness last long, and is the parent over-identifying with the youngster? This means taking a step back so as not to saturate the child with one's own anxieties.

This book is about "mind" over "what's the matter." Understanding the relationship between child and parent [or parents] ensures a building from the outside in so that eventual problem solving comes from the building blocks in family ties. The book teaches parents how to work with several systems: the family environment, the ecology of the home [and] school community, and the other helpers. The wide range of more benign to severe anxiety conditions is described, with various remedies for parents to follow as needed.

This book is a helpful guide, applicable to children and adolescents, and it can be taken off the shelf many times as children progress though their development."

—CARL BAGNINI, LCSW, BCD

Senior faculty, International Psychotherapy Institute, Washington, DC and Long Island, NY teaching child and family therapy, couple therapy and psychoanalytic supervision

"In her excellent book *Unlocking Parental Intelligence: Finding Meaning in Your Child's Behavior*, Dr. Hollman encouraged parents to seek out the meaning of their child or teen's misbehavior before trying to deal with it. She showed parents how to pause and reflect on their thoughts and feelings about the situation and how to think about their child's possibly different thoughts and feelings and his or her developmental level. She explained how understanding the meaning of their child's behavior enables parents to empathically resolve problem behaviors.

This new book is a superb follow-up that provides a short, practical guide for parents struggling to help their anxious child or teen. Dr. Hollman summarizes the Parental Intelligence principles and gives insightful real-world examples of the principles in action with anxious children. The book is a quick, easy read that offers real help for managing different kinds of anxiety in children and teens. Highly recommended!

—JANET WILDE ASTINGTON, PHD

Professor Emeritus. Institute of Child Study, Department of Human Development and Applied Psychology, University of Toronto; Editor, *Minds in the Making*

"Dr. Hollman builds upon the impressive foundation she established in *Unlocking Parental Intelligence: Finding Meaning in Your Child's Behavior* by focusing on challenges parents encounter with children's specific types of anxiety. Dr. Hollman guides parents in utilizing her proactive and empathic stepwise approach to foster collaboration with their children in clarifying and managing their anxiety, while enhancing parents' and children's sense of self-efficacy, and fortifying family bonds that will likely endure for generations to come.

An outstanding practical guide for all parents and professionals."

—LYNN SESKIN, PSYD

Clinical and School Psychologist

"Dr. Laurie Hollman's book on helping your child manage anxiety will be very helpful in responding to one of the challenges of being a parent. Her book provides parents with an insightful approach to their children's difficulties through understanding their children's actions as well as reflecting on their own reactions. She illustrates her approach with excellent examples of working out how to help children overcome their anxiety. This book has the potential to improve parent's and their children's lives."

—JEREMY CARPENDALE, PHD

Professor of Developmental Psychology, Department of Psychology, Simon Fraser University, Burnaby, BC V5A 1S6 Canada

The
BUSY PARENT'S
GUIDE to MANAGING
ANXIETY
IN CHILDREN
AND TEENS

THE PARENTAL INTELLIGENCE WAY

FAMILIUS

Copyright © 2018 by Laurie Hollman
All rights reserved.
Published by Familius LLC, www.familius.com

Familius books are available at special discounts for bulk purchases, whether
for sales promotions or for family or corporate use. For more information,
contact Familius Sales at 559-876-2170 or email orders@familius.com.

Library of Congress Cataloging-in-Publication Data
2018934005

Print ISBN 9781641700108
Ebook ISBN 9781641700559

Printed in the United States of America

Edited by Brooke Jorden
Cover design by David Miles
Book design by Brooke Jorden

10 9 8 7 6 5 4 3 2 1
First Edition

LAURIE HOLLMAN, PhD

The
BUSY PARENT'S
GUIDE to MANAGING
ANXIETY
IN CHILDREN
AND TEENS

A QUICK READ
FOR POWERFUL
SOLUTIONS!

THE PARENTAL INTELLIGENCE WAY

To Jeff, for his loving empathy
and compassion as a husband
and father.

ACKNOWLEDGMENTS

I am thankful for all those who have inspired and helped me with this book. First and foremost, I am grateful to my husband, Jeff, my partner in life, for his unending support of my ongoing writing about parenting. He has always strengthened my resolve to put my ideas into words. My gratitude also goes to my sons, David and Rich, who were raised with Parental Intelligence and continue to discuss my concepts and support their evolution. I would also like to thank Claire, David's wife, my wonderful daughter-in-law, for her continual enthusiasm and encouragement of my work.

With pleasure, I give thanks to the delightful staff at Familius for publishing my books, including founder and president Christopher Robbins, who supports his authors so well, and David Miles for his artistic book covers.

Particularly at Familius, I am appreciative of my gifted editor, Brooke Jorden, whose devotion to her work and expertise as a writer has enhanced my book and brought it to fruition. I am further grateful to Leah Welker, who also edited this book with talent and effectiveness.

In addition, I thank the many parents and their children and adolescents in my practice over the years who inspired my desire to write this book so others could benefit from their courage in building strong parent-child and parent-adolescent ties.

As my psychoanalytic training and research has progressed throughout the many years of my practice, I am grateful to the voices of so many others who have influenced me and broadened and deepened my psychological knowledge.

I conclude by thanking my loving grandsons—Zander, age 9, and Eddie, age 7, at the time I wrote this book—for their impressive insights into how children think and feel. Their wondrous ability to put their ideas into words supports and inspires my belief in young children's capacities to be empathic and capable problem solvers. When they confide in me their personal thoughts and wishes, I am reminded of the essence of Parental Intelligence: the close bonds it brings between parent and child, grandparent and grandchild.

CONTENTS

INTRODUCTION 1

CHAPTER ONE: THE PARENTAL INTELLIGENCE WAY 7

CHAPTER TWO: GENERALIZED ANXIETY 25

CHAPTER THREE: PANIC ATTACKS 37

CHAPTER FOUR: OBSESSIVE-COMPULSIVE DISORDER 53

CHAPTER FIVE: SEPARATION ANXIETY 67

REVIEW AND ADDITIONAL REMARKS:
    RESOLVING THE PARENT-CHILD ANXIETY SPIRAL
    AND ENJOYING LIFE 81

INTRODUCTION

*D*o you wonder why your child or teen seems on edge, unduly nervous, or restless at times—maybe all of the time? Are you uncertain if and when you should be worried? Are you so busy that sometimes you dismiss these thoughts but later reconsider them? You may be noticing that you have an anxious child or teen.

In my psychotherapy practice, parents have taught me that anxiety is a difficult state of mind to help their children manage, modify, and eventually master—but it is not impossible. This book hopes to address those challenges to help parents understand and manage the behavior and feelings of children and teens with both fleeting and chronic anxiety.

It's important to distinguish fear from anxiety. Fear is the reaction to real or perceived actual danger, whereas anxiety is a disproportionate vigilant response to the anticipation of a future threat that may lead to avoidant behavior. When someone is fearful, they have a fight-or-flight reaction with thoughts of immediate danger requiring escape. Anxiety is more often related to muscle tension and a wary, watchful, sometimes overwhelming cautious attitude.

Most kids feel worried and anxious periodically as they encounter new experiences and challenges. An anxiety disorder, however, features excessive fear, often related to behavioral disturbances that persist beyond normal developmental stages. For example, we expect a toddler to be anxious momentarily when his mother leaves the room. He is not yet fully certain that what he can't see is still there. So, he follows her and reassures himself she is still at home. However, should an elementary school child or teenager do the same, we would find it abnormal and worrisome, requiring intervention to help us understand the underlying causes and the remedies.

It's common to suffer along with your anxious child and feel that parenting is beyond you, as if it requires a special kind of intelligence that wasn't encrypted on your brain. I have been inspired to write this book after thirty years as a psychoanalyst working with mothers and fathers who came to me at different stages in their parenting careers, questioning how to help their anxious kids. They were all searching for that special intelligence needed for such parenting, even if they didn't quite know how to ask for it.

Ever since I wrote the Gold Mom's Choice Award book, *Unlocking Parental Intelligence: Finding Meaning in Your Child's Behavior*, parents and professionals have requested that I write some short, practical books applying the Parental Intelligence method to the specific challenges parents face, such as managing anxiety in their kids. Parental Intelligence is an approach to parenting that gives busy parents an organized, reliable way to attend to these varied situations, whether they are minimal or excessive.

I coined the term *Parental Intelligence* because I believe parents who are willing to pause and reflect before they react can find many of the answers and insights they need within themselves. Parenting anxious kids, specifically, requires you to understand that anxiety is an emotional state that reveals meaningful thoughts and feelings that you can ultimately learn to decipher. This new, enlightening perspective, gained through Parental Intelligence, can be such a relief! As you continue to practice this process, you will become a *meaning-maker*, empowered to read the thoughts and feelings underlying your child's anxiety like an open book. Once you understand what is going through your child's or teen's mind, you can collaborate with them to solve their problems. This not only relieves anxiety but also strengthens the parent-child bond.

The types of situations that produce anxiety or avoidance behaviors—and the thoughts and worries that accompany these intense emotions—will vary from disorder to disorder and from child to child. With Parental Intelligence, you will figure out the *whys* behind your child's anxious responses. With Parental Intelligence, you enter the inner world of your child or teen and understand where he or she is coming from. As you try to calm your upset child or teen in the moment, you may only focus on lessening the immediate anxiety, but to help your child manage these feelings in the long run, you will first need to understand each episode's meaning and even consider it a message and an invitation to empathic understanding.

In this book, I will describe the five steps to Parental Intelligence that provide the tools you need to approach your child's anxiety using multiple examples. I will offer specific suggestions that you can implement to help your child cope with anxious states of mind and understand the meanings behind these complex emotional experiences. It is my hope that the straightforward information provided in this book will help prevent anxiety from escalating and offer reassurance for busy parents like you when you feel uncertain, leaving you free to enjoy the pleasures of helping your children and teens grow and develop.

The chapters are arranged to explain and illustrate common anxiety disorders: generalized anxiety, panic disorders, obsessive-compulsive disorders, and separation anxiety. I will describe the key features of each disorder for children and for teens. Common to these different disorders or normal periodic anxiety is that the child or teen overestimates the danger in a situation and draws erroneous conclusions that cause him or her excessive worry, which then induces some or all autonomic physical reactions: general uneasiness, restlessness, "butterflies" in the stomach, trembling, chest pain, tension in the child's facial expressions or posture, and racing thoughts with rapid or confused speech.

In order to preserve the privacy of my patients and the people I've come across in daily life who deal with anxiety in all these forms, I have written fictionalized accounts of anxiety in children and adolescents and associated family dynamics. These stories demonstrate how each situation can be managed and resolved using Parental Intelligence, and the result is a closer parent-child bond and greater overall understanding. Parental Intelligence provides the busy parent not only a structured approach to helping anxious kids but also a vision of hope—an avenue for parents to better understand their children at all ages and developmental levels, firming up and fortifying the parent-child and parent-teen relationships. Using Parental Intelligence, parents support their anxious kids as they help them solve their problems and lead loving, satisfying lives.

CHAPTER ONE

THE
PARENTAL INTELLIGENCE WAY

Ten-year-old Lidia is drumming her fingers on her cheek as she stares at her homework. She has a worried expression on her face with a furrowed brow and pursed lips. She seems disorganized with papers scattered about. Her mother notices but is preoccupied with getting dinner prepared before Lidia's father comes home to relieve her of her parental activities; she will be the keynote speaker at a fundraiser tonight and cannot be late. She is a busy woman, barely getting home on time from work to get everything done. *Oh, no,* she thinks, glancing sideways at her daughter, *she's as anxious as ever—about what this time, I don't know. But I do know I don't have time for a chat. What's a mother to do anyway with a chronically anxious kid?*

Lidia starts to cry, quietly at first, but soon she is bawling. Head down, she is clearly distraught. Her mother tells her to have her snack and do her homework later. This would give her time to settle down. Always wanting to listen to her mother, she controls herself and goes upstairs, only to resume her stream of tears when she's alone. Her body is trembling and her throat is dry. She hates that her mother is going out; the thought triggers her separation anxiety.

Let's replay this situation, only this time, Lidia's mother uses Parental Intelligence, a different approach that allows her to be more empathic and proactive. Notice the shift in Lidia's mother's attitude and how her daughter responds gratefully.

Seeing her daughter in obvious distress, Lidia's mother steps back in her mind to see if she could imagine what this was about. She's tempted to rush in, but she wants to give Lidia some time to regulate her emotions on her own. When clearly this isn't happening, she sits by her, puts her arm around her, and asks, "Sweetheart, what's the matter? Something going wrong today?"

Lidia nods, still crying. "I didn't make the second cut on the lacrosse team." To her mother, this doesn't seem too disastrous, but to Lidia, at ten years old, it means not being in the popular crowd. "And my hair frizzed up because of the rain and that awful Leslie teased me and she *did* make second cut."

Lidia's mother's heart breaks for her while still feeling on edge herself about her presentation that night. She wants to know more about what is on Lidia's mind because she is a very well-liked kid. "Tell me more about this situation."

"Well," said Lidia, "it means next year I won't make the travel team, and that's a way to get a scholarship for college."

"College! That's years away. You have a superb academic record and surely will by high school. Do you think we can take things one at a time? Next term, you can try out again."

Given that reasonable perspective, Lidia's tears recede and she gives her mother a big hug. "I don't feel so dizzy anymore, and my chest isn't pounding now. Phew! I thought I'd never feel better."

Now Lidia's mother knew: her daughter had been having a panic attack. *No wonder she was crying so hard*, she thinks. *She must've been really scared. Thank goodness she's calm so her separation anxiety won't kick in when I go out.*

What a difference! How did this busy mother turn a possible disaster into a learning and bonding moment with her daughter and prevent a full-blown panic attack? The answer is simple: she used Parental Intelligence. In just fifteen minutes, mother and daughter were settled down. Lidia began her homework, Mother made dinner, and Dad came home in time. Parental Intelligence gave this busy woman the tools to keep her daughter from slipping over the edge unnecessarily. Let's look more closely at how this works.

FIVE STEPS TO PARENTAL INTELLIGENCE

What is Parental Intelligence? While individual parents all face unique challenges, I have discovered many commonalities that affect their varied situations. I have developed five powerfully valuable steps that allow every parent—no matter how different their circumstances—to quickly and effectively find meaning behind their child or teen's anxiety and, beyond that, to intelligently and compassionately resolve the underlying problems. This process builds Parental Intelligence.

The five steps to Parental Intelligence are:

1. Stepping Back
2. Self-Reflecting

WUTSCHKE, MELANIE

Unclaim : 3/16/2020

Held date   : 3/9/2020
Pickup location : Hillsboro Brookwood Library

Title   : The busy parent's guide to man
aging anxiety in children and teens : a quick re
ad for powerful solutions! : the parental intell
igence way
Call number   : PAR 649.154 HOLLMAN
Item barcode   : 33614075441443
Assigned branch : Bethany Library

Notes:

3. Understanding Your Child's Mind
4. Understanding Your Child's Development
5. Problem Solving

Together, these five steps provide a road map to help you get to your destination: the place where you understand the meaning behind your child's anxiety. (*Child* refers to your son or daughter at any age, from toddler to teenager.) What was once obscure will become clear. When the meaning or meanings behind the anxiety are understood, it is much easier to decide the best ways to handle the situation.

Going through the five-step process with your child or teen often uncovers problems that are of greater significance than the original anxiety. What had previously been unspeakable will become known, and a new and stronger alliance will form between you and your child.

While lots of parents are just looking for quick-fix answers, learning this five-step process allows them to apply it quickly and automatically every time an anxiety incident arises. It's an organized parenting approach that resolves anxiety effectively by calming the child down as rapidly as is feasible, depending on the circumstances. Ultimately, parents become more compassionate and efficient problem solvers, actually saving a lot of time that they might have spent guessing with trial-and-error parenting.

STEP ONE
Stepping Back

A parent's first reaction to seeing their child or teen filled with anxiety is often emotional. Without distancing themselves from their emotional response, parents often make rash decisions that they later regret because they do not achieve the desired results. Responding effectively may be uncomfortable, but making it a priority to step back, tolerate the child's feelings, and gradually shift to a more reasoned response will lead to a better outcome.

Sometimes parents refrain from acting impulsively but feel a nagging tension that interferes with their ability to see the situation objectively. Such a parent may be stuck in one point of view or focus solely on a specific but incomplete set of details. It is not always enough to replay an event, because the replay may confirm or intensify the original emotion.

The process of stepping back includes the suspension of judgment. This allows you to take time to figure out what happened before taking action. If you never pause, you never allow emotions to subside and thinking to begin. Stepping back prepares you to engage in the parenting mindset that says what happened is meaningful. Even in an emergency, once the immediate situation has been handled, there is room for refraining from ready conclusions and for stepping back.

Stepping back requires slowing down and thinking about what just happened and how you feel about it—suspending judgment about not only your child's behavior but also your parenting behavior.

Stepping back gives the parent permission to not always know what to do. Consequently, when a parent reacts one way on the spot, but later understands what happened more fully, he or she can feel confident returning to the child with new thoughts and feelings that, though once restricted, have begun to expand, offering a new perspective.

When you step back, you prepare yourself to recognize that anxiety has many causes. By pausing, you give yourself time to compare the last time anxiety surfaced to the present situation. You may discover a pattern in your interaction with your child and begin to wonder, *Are there many causes for the anxiety that I didn't consider at the time?* You may then begin to see the anxiety in its many aspects: What triggered the anxiety? How long did it last? When did it escalate or decrease? You may also begin to see facets of the anxiety you were blind to because of your child's and your own high emotional states during the incident. Once you are in the mode of seeking full knowledge of what happened, you will begin to discover that several factors might be involved. Once you calm down, you begin to notice expressions on your child's face, the words your child said, your child's gestures and postures, and your child's mood and shifts in feelings.

Stepping back gives you space and time to evaluate the situation, examine and question assumptions, and realize that the situation isn't fully understood. Take as much time as you need to consider what is happening. In your mind, say to yourself, *Slo-o-o-w down. Take your time. Hold on. Don't rush forward. Resist those impulses. Breathe deeply. Sit quietly. Consider what to say or do, if anything.*

STEP TWO
Self-Reflecting

Self-reflecting allows you to discover how your past affects your present approach to parenting. Self-reflecting allows you to observe yourself objectively and think about the genesis of your feelings, motives, and actions in both present and previous relationships. It's so tempting to just jump to solutions and skip questioning what's going on inside of you.

For parents, self-reflecting is an extension of stepping back. It requires you to consider what led to your specific initial emotional responses to your child's anxiety, prompts you to think about your actions from many perspectives, and allows you to consider many causes for your responses to your child. You begin to question, *Why did I react that specific way, now that I see it wasn't the only way? What were my motives and intentions? What in my past affected my thinking and actions in the present? What were my emotional reactions to my child's behavior, and where did they come from?*

When Lidia's mother reacted to Lidia in the second version of the vignette, she had taken some time to self-reflect on her own experiences of anxiety. In fact, her own anxiety about the impending fundraiser instantly alerted her to what Lidia might be going through. Doing so, she was then able to help her daughter to decrease her nervous state of mind lovingly and effectively.

If you allow yourself to take your time, this isn't as difficult as you might imagine. In fact, you notice that you're beginning to feel more confident. Self-reflecting is a discovery process. You are getting to know yourself better.

There are several possibilities. If your child's behavior, manner, posture, or tone of voice resonate with how you interacted with someone else at earlier times in your life, you may be reacting to your child the way you reacted when you were younger. That's very enlightening. Or you may be reacting to your child the way you wished you had reacted when you were younger. Your mind is racing backward, and you are feeling much more in touch with your reactions. Alternatively, it may be that someone reacted to you the way your child is behaving now, and that is what's so upsetting to you. Past and present have converged. No wonder you reacted so strongly.

STEP THREE
Understanding Your Child's Mind

"What's on your mind?" is a question often asked casually, but understanding your child or teen's mind is central to knowing them. Understanding your child's mind starts with knowing your child's mental states, including intentions, thoughts, desires, wishes, beliefs, and feelings. Be aware that contradictory and diverse mental states can occur at the same time.

Your ability to understand your child's mind is directly related to your ability to self-reflect. As described above, self-reflecting is your capacity to think about your own experiences throughout life. Self-awareness and awareness of the mental states of others are closely linked. When, with self-reflecting, you are able to understand how your own mind is working, you also realize that your child's mind is separate and autonomous from yours. However, if you do not understand this, you may unknowingly attribute your own mental states (intentions and feelings) to your child.

Most parents and children can recognize each other's moods but need time to figure out the reason for a particular mood. Anxious behavior is meaningful, even if you don't catch on right away. Of course, it's important to check your ideas with your child. This shows empathy: "It seems like your feelings were hurt by the teacher, so you got nervous and bolted out of the classroom. Was it something like that?"

Let's say your child reveals she is feeling hurt. After hearing your child's response, you might continue: "Now that we can figure out what was going on in your mind, were there other choices you may have had, so that you can react another way next time you feel hurt?"

No one likes being instructed on how they should feel, but it sure feels good to be understood. Everyone appreciates empathy. Feeling understood can help a child contain his emotions and begin to think them through. When a child feels his parent understands what is going on inside his mind, he feels attended to and supported, and then can think further about how to handle situations.

What does understanding your child's mind have to do with empathy? Parents find that practicing empathic understanding gives them insight into their child's mind. For example, parents form an idea of what their child might be feeling when the child verbally says something or physically does something in particular that alerts the parent to the child's distress. It's like trying to step into your child's shoes and see from his or her point of view.

Verbal communication is only one piece of the puzzle. In addition to what your child says, watch your child's facial expressions and body language to get an idea of what's on his or her mind. Anxious kids may have a furrowed brow, a twitching eye, or crinkled lines at the edges of eyes and may be running their fingers through their hair. Speech, of course, helps us understand the other's mind, but silences, stiffening or tightening of muscles, and facial expressions are also meaningful.

Sometimes we are blind to an emotion in our children that we block out in ourselves. For instance, an anxious parent who blocks out hurt may be blind to his or her child's hurt. Thus, parents can misperceive what they feel, thinking they feel only one emotion (anxiety) while truly feeling something more (hurt).

If this is true, then recognizing your child's hurt might lead to you feeling your own, the result of self-reflecting. If you don't know what is on your own mind—what you are thinking and feeling—you may subsequently be blocked from understanding what is on your child's mind—what he or she is thinking and feeling. You may draw erroneous conclusions.

Trying to understand your children's minds shows them you believe in them and teaches them to believe in themselves. Treating your children like capable human beings with well-functioning minds and good intentions builds trust.

STEP FOUR
Understanding Your Child's Development

There are developmental stages at which children master different skills, but not all children reach those stages at the same time. For example, your seven-year-old may be more adept at completing a math problem than a nine-year-old. Your thirteen-year-old may be more empathic than a sixteen-year-old. Two children in the same grade may perform differently on the same assignment.

The age when a child reaches a certain skill level is the child's *developmental age* for that skill, regardless of the child's chronological age. When parents take into account the developmental age of their child—which reflects the stage the child has reached in mastering certain capacities—parents and children get along better.

What capacities should you look for? Notice your child's interpersonal skills: impulse control, effective communication, empathy, and thinking or cognition. Watch for the development of individual capacities such as autonomy, identity formation, and self-reliance.

You'll probably find your children aren't consistent across the board; they have strengths and weaknesses. The chronological age may not be the same as the developmental age for any of these capacities, and children may be at different developmental levels for different skills. When you set expectations for your children, be sure they reflect each child's developmental levels, which may fall behind or step ahead of their chronological age.

Ask two questions: *What is expected at my child's stage of development?* and *How far apart is my child's chronological age from my child's developmental age?* Being critical of a child for not completing tasks expected for their chronological age creates anxiety. Expectations that do not reflect your child's developmental age won't be met and will create acute emotional distress. Healthcare providers such as pediatricians discuss child development at yearly check-ups. Teachers, social workers, and psychologists also discuss child development in parent conferences in schools. These interventions keep the parent in tune with what to expect for their particular child. If the child's anxiety isn't just occasional and fleeting, healthcare workers and teachers will notice the chronicity of the anxiety and want to discuss this emotional problem with the parent. Once the parent and others are aware of the child's anxiety, they can work together to relieve and remedy the problem.

STEP FIVE
Problem Solving

The more you continue working on the first four steps, the more natural they will become, getting you ready for the last step: problem solving. Interestingly, by now, the initial problem, the specific anxiety, has become part of a set of problems to be solved over time. The immediate importance of the initial anxiety may have lessened because it has been recognized as a symptom of more pressing issues lying underneath. These are the problems you ultimately hope to solve, together with your child, using Parental Intelligence.

Problem solving aims to find mutual meanings, which may be new to both participants. Meanings are exchanged through taking collaborative turns in talking things out in order to correct misinterpretations of the anxious behavior in question. Parent and child learn new coping skills that can be used in the future.

The steps in this book that lead to problem solving are based on your desire to have a strong, healthy, and joyful relationship with your child.

Without a good relationship, problems are rarely solved. The steps leading from stepping back to problem solving seem linear, but you may need to go back and forth among them. This is truly significant because the earlier steps bear directly on the process of problem solving.

While problem solving, you may realize you need to be more reflective about your view of reality and your child's view of reality. If, indeed, you and your child can see the problem from each other's points of view, both you and your child should be ready to problem solve together. In other words, for problem solving to become possible and effective, you need to try to understand what is on both your mind and your child's mind. You need to view the situation not only from your point of view but also from your child's vantage point. If you can do so and share your understanding with your child, your child will be prompted to reciprocate. If you and your child can't comprehend and picture each other's reality you can't solve a problem together.

Problem solving is a relational process that involves give and take. When children learn that their parents realize the underlying problems behind their original anxiety, they become more open than ever to hearing what their parents have to say because they are feeling understood. Children are relieved to know their mother or father is open to their points of view, wants to hear about their feelings, and is aware of the developmental struggles they may be going through.

CHAPTER TWO

GENERALIZED ANXIETY

*T*all, brown-haired Clive is a likable seven-year-old kid with an engaging disposition. Developmentally, he is on par with kids his age. He has great traits: spunk, independence, a good sense of responsibility, reasonable self-reliance, and a quick wit. However, he suffers with persistent and excessive anxiety and worries about all kinds of activities, even ordinary routine stuff like getting on the school bus, performing academically, getting his teachers' and parents' approval, and baseball. He actually does above average or excels in all these activities. His worry is out of proportion to the actual circumstances and is difficult to control and even affects him physically. He feels restless and on edge from the time he wakes up in the morning. He is easily tired after not sleeping well and irritable with muscle tension and difficulty concentrating. His concerns shift rapidly from one to another, and some anxious episodes have lasted more than six months.

His mother knows he has an overanxious disorder and has been grappling with it for a long time. She knows his worries are excessive and affect his everyday life in a pervasive and pronounced way, often without clear precipitants. He is restless; she can tell he is keyed up and on edge much of the time. She knows he's particularly distressed when, like she sees today, he is twitching a bit, feeling shaky, and has muscle aches. It's clear to her that her son is troubled. His worries are age appropriate but disproportionate to the realities of his daily life. His mother is a busy woman, but she helps Clive by using Parental Intelligence. These steps calm him when certain triggers stir him up. She knows this is a familial trait; she has generalized anxiety as well. Having coped with it for many years, she feels competent to help him.

Today he came home from school worried about his spelling test; he had earned a B instead of his usual

A. She steps back and watches to see how it is affecting him. He is staring at that spelling test with a tense look. While it makes her nervous to see him so unnecessarily worried, she gives him a chance to calm down on his own. Seeing that it is interfering with his doing his other assignments, she decides a chat is in order to understand what is on his mind.

"Clive, you seem upset about the spelling test; I see you are staring at it. Do you need me to sign it?"

"Yes. I can't believe I missed three words out of twenty and got a B grade. I studied hard and just got distracted and wrote the wrong letters. I'm such a failure."

"You feel like a failure because of one B after tons of A's? Does that make real sense to you or do you think it's out of proportion?"

Clive takes a deep breath. "When you put it that way, my heart beats slower. If you can be so calm about it, I guess I just messed up. Maybe it's not such a terrible thing after all. The teacher never even said a word. Would you sign it?"

"Sure. It's important to remember that you have this tendency to think something is awful when it's ordinary. Everyone makes mistakes now and then, even great students like you. Does that make sense to you?"

"Yeah. Now I'll be able to concentrate on the other homework I have and sleep okay tonight. Thanks!"

This whole conversation took only a few minutes and Clive regained control of his emotions. The problem remained, however, that his anxiety level could quickly climb in reaction to something else. He had trouble keeping perspective without his mother's help. In this instance, however, clarifying Clive's belief that he was a global failure seemed to put him on the right track. Learning not to jump to conclusions is a lesson that will continue to help him ease his anxiety in other situations. His mother will probably have to repeat this notion many times until he absorbs it and recognizes himself when he does it. Quickly reacting negatively is common for anxious kids like Clive, so his mother was wise to address that style of thinking.

TIPS FOR PARENTS OF CHILDREN WITH OVERANXIOUS DISORDERS

1. Refer to the steps of Parental Intelligence so your own reactions don't stir up but instead calm down your child.
2. Speak in quiet, even, gentle tones to your anxious child so he absorbs the tenor of your voice and internalizes it to combat his racing thoughts.

3. Listen attentively to what is on your child's mind. Remind him that his ideas are out of proportion to the event at hand and that together you can come up with ways to solve whatever problem he perceives at the moment.

4. Listen for his own ideas for coping with the anxiety before offering advice so he develops coping mechanisms he can use when you're not around.

5. Coping mechanisms that help a child regain perspective can include breathing slowly and deeply, consciously slowing thoughts, reviewing the situation and asking yourself if your ideas are out of proportion to the situation, and/or telling an adult (teacher, coach, parent) about your worries to get their perspective to counteract your own.

6. Parents can inform teachers, guidance counselors, and other school staff such as social workers and psychologists that their child is overanxious and may need to be calmed down during the day. As the child hears the calm from such adults as well as parents, he can slowly internalize others' points of view that will counteract his instant and unnecessary worry.

Teenagers similarly can have general anxiety. The major difference is that their concerns are different from when they were younger. Fifteen-year-old Lia, for example, worries about fitting into social groups, performing well academically (because she has concerns about getting into college), having the approval of her parents and various teachers regarding her performance, and succumbing to peer pressures to try drugs and sex that she knows will only make her more anxious.

One afternoon, Lia came home from school with a tense expression on her face. Her forehead was creased and tight, her shoulders constricted, and her gait fast and hurried. Her mother witnessed this posture and waited patiently to see if it eased or escalated. She knew these were typical of a child with anxiety. When Lia went to her room and stayed alone for almost an hour without even taking her snack, her mother knew that something was putting her on edge. She was usually starving after school, especially after a swim meet with her team. Controlling her own apprehension, she quietly knocked on Lia's door and asked if she wanted her snack. When Lia said she had no appetite, her mother asked to come in to her room. Lia consented hesitantly, fearing her mother's reaction to her worries.

"How was your day? You seem a bit on edge."

"Oh, it's the usual. I wasn't invited to the popular kids' sleepover. No one likes me. I don't want to make a big deal about it, but why do they leave me out?" Her whole body seemed to be trembling and her eyes were teary.

"Didn't you go to a sleepover just last week at Clara's house? Don't you think she likes you?"

"Yes, she does and the other five girls there were lots of fun, but they aren't the most popular. I'm so confused. The popular girls don't even get good grades, which would bother me, but they hang so close, gossip terribly, and ignore the rest of us. I actually don't get it why the boys seem to like them so much. I wish I had a boyfriend. Maybe I never will."

"You seem kind of critical of them and yourself. Are you sure you want to be a part of a group with these girls? They don't seem very nice and who knows what their relationships really are like with boys. Popularity is relative, don't you think? There's plenty of time to begin dating, and there are different circles of girls. But, this one sleepover seems to have affected your self-esteem."

"It's true. I forget all the good things and focus on the negatives. Talking sure helps. My body is calmer now. I really did enjoy the sleepover I went to, and they are nicer girls. They aren't nasty and judgmental about other kids, and they do like me and we like to do the same stuff. We were laughing all night and staying up late that I know is okay with you. I do worry that I'm not part of the 'in group,' but you don't really seem to care, and that makes me more comfortable with not needing them. I wish I didn't jump to conclusions so quickly. I should realize that the girls I have the most in common with should really be my friends. "

"It's great that you noticed that about yourself. I like you to have whatever friends make you feel cared about. It's not important how many friends you have, just that there's a mutual sharing of feelings and interests. The girls you hang out with seem to like to read the same books, ride bikes, and some are on the swim team with you. Sounds really great, honestly."

Lia takes a long deep breath, smiles, and hugs her mother, who feels her daughter's body tension ease up considerably. She even reaches for her snack. Her appetite has returned.

The reason Lia's mother was effective was because she and Lia have built up a trusting relationship over many years. Lia didn't come right out with her concerns because she didn't want her mother to think less of her for being anxious. Unfortunately, she is ashamed that she struggles with anxiety. Her closest girlfriends know and accept this about her, which is so important. When she gained her perspective back, she knew that popularity was really a myth with regard to how likable she was. With her mother's reassurance, her self-esteem climbed back up and she felt better. Lia understood that her ideas were out of proportion to reality and that she sometimes jumped to conclusions. This was a big step for her to recognize this by herself.

TIPS FOR PARENTS OF ANXIOUS TEENS

1. Follow the steps to Parental Intelligence to relate successfully with your child.
2. Enter your teen's world slowly and nonjudgmentally because she worries not only about events in her daily life, but also about your opinion of them.
3. Praise her own ability to see things realistically to ease excessive worry by recognizing when she makes events seem bigger and more important than they are.
4. Just as with younger kids, parents need to always speak calmly themselves, so the teenager can internalize that calm voice inside herself.
5. If needed, lead your teen through a relaxation exercise: Tell her to relax her neck, shoulders, chest, buttocks, legs, and feet. Sometimes

hearing these instructions from someone else is more effective than doing it yourself and interrupting the process by returning to your worries. Listening to quiet music helps as well.

6. If the anxiety persists for months, consider suggesting to your teen that she talk to a therapist trained to treat anxiety once or twice a week.

7. Teenagers also can benefit from psychotropic medications that ease their anxiety if talking is not sufficient. The therapist can recommend an adolescent psychopharmacologist to make that assessment.

8. The bottom line is a good, mutually trusting parent-teen relationship. When teenagers know their parents will listen non-critically to them—there is much less pushback and rebellion. They know their parents are their allies. This eases anxiety all by itself.

HOW DO PARENTS KNOW WHEN ANXIETY IS NORMAL OR ABNORMAL?

Lia showed social anxiety anticipating an upcoming social situation she felt excluded from. She felt evaluated by her peers and had excessive worry about a future event: the sleepover with "popular" kids.

Social and performance anxiety are common among teenagers. Performance anxiety usually pertains to grades, the anticipation of preparing to enter college, and athletic events. This anxiety is considered abnormal only if it is persistently excessive. Muscle tension and feeling keyed up, on edge, with difficulty concentrating and sleeping are common symptoms of anxiety that undermine confidence in teens. It can't be stressed enough that a sound parent-child relationship is central to internalizing a calmer inner voice and increasing the teen's self-confidence and effective performance in and out of school.

The anxiety is abnormal only if it lasts more than six months and is excessive. Excessive worrying impairs the teen's capacity to do things effectively at home and school. The worrying itself is tiring and takes up time and energy. Excessive anxiety is recognizable if it is free-floating, meaning that it easily gets attached to ordinary situations, often moving from one event to another on a regular basis. These kids often have sleep disturbances because they can't calm their restless minds and this nighttime problem, along with the exhaustion that comes with worrying, interferes with the teen's general functioning.

CHAPTER THREE

PANIC ATTACKS

anic attacks are times of intense fear without realistic danger that typically last from a few minutes up to approximately thirty minutes. Symptoms may include chest pain, palpitations, trembling, sweating, muscle tension, numbness, disorientation, and a feeling of impending dread as if something bad is about to happen. Panic attacks are relatively rare in children until puberty when the prevalence may increase (*Diagnostic and Statistical Manual of Mental Disorders, Fifth Edition*, 210).

However, there are always exceptions, such as nine-year-old Eva.

Eva is a charming, kind little girl with long, curly hair and a sturdy build. She is average in school, which is acceptable to her generally because she focuses more on having friends and other activities. She likes softball, gymnastics, and drawing, and meets her parents' expectations for performing at school and at home. She does her chores usually, complaining now and then like a typical kid.

However, Eva suffers with recurrent, unexpected panic attacks just like her dad. She'll have an abrupt surge of intense fear or discomfort that peaks within a few minutes during which time several symptoms occur: her heart rate accelerates, she sweats, and she often shakes. She feels like she's short of breath, almost like choking. Sometimes she feels nauseated and dizzy, sometimes like she'll faint (she never does). The worst part is she feels like she's going crazy. Because this has happened many times, she lives in fear of the attacks recurring. During the attacks, she fears they'll never end, which only increases her anxiety and makes the attack last longer. Sometimes she avoids situations that she thinks may lead to an attack, such as big tests in school. On those days, she complains about stomachaches, which she feels even though she isn't sick; they are caused by the increased anxiety.

One weekend, Eva and her dad are in the grocery store shopping for ingredients for the next week's meals. Seemingly out of nowhere, Eva begins to get nervous, grabs her dad's hand, and goes into a full panic attack. Having had them himself, he quickly recognizes the symptoms as his trembling daughter seems to be getting disoriented. He can tell that Eva, like many children who experience panic attacks, is starting to lose touch with reality, forgetting that she was just in a grocery store.

She says, "Hold on, Dad. I'm going crazy again. I feel so dizzy," and she begins to sweat.

Dad stops shopping, grabs her hand, and says reassuringly, "You are having an anxiety attack, and we will slow it down together. Cover your mouth and nose with your hands and breathe slowly. It will last a short time, and you'll soon be back to yourself."

Trusting her dad, as they'd been through this process before, she listens to his deep, calm voice carefully and her breathing slows, her heart rate decelerates rapidly. The smothering feeling goes away slowly but surely as she prevents herself from feeling overwhelmed and scared. All of these tactics work, and soon enough, she is back to herself. But she wants to leave the store. She and her dad leave their cart and walk slowly, hand in hand, back to the car.

Eva's father used Parental Intelligence instantly. He stepped back and gave himself and his daughter time to relieve the symptoms without understanding why they occurred. Nothing particularly obvious had happened in the store to trigger the attack. However, he must continue to use the steps of Parental Intelligence after the episode to understand Eva, uncover the root of the problem, and learn how to help her in the future.

Once in the car, they just sit and wait. Dad feels himself relaxing. He had become apprehensive in the store but shielded his daughter from seeing his emotions when they surged forward. It's really tough to see your child go through such an attack so unexpectedly.

Staying in the car, they drive to a nearby park, get out, and sit together on the grass. Stepping back and self-reflecting had worked, but it was time to understand something of what might be on Eva's mind.

"How are you feeling now, Eva?" Dad asks.

"So much better. I really felt like it wouldn't end, but what you said focused me and those scary feelings went away. Phew! I'm glad it's sunny out. Thanks for leaving the store. I felt too closed in being there for some reason."

"I understand," says Dad. "Let's think about what's been on your mind these past few days."

"Well, thinking back, while we were shopping, I did start to worry about all the homework I have that I should have done after school on Friday, but put off and now it's Saturday and tomorrow is Sunday and we have a lot planned to do and I don't know when I'll get to finish it. The math is the hardest for me and I don't want to disappoint my teacher this year—I really like her. I don't know why I thought about it in the grocery store except that maybe instead of coming with you I should've stayed home and done my homework."

"So I guess, underneath the fun of shopping, your anxiety was hanging out inside your mind about this schoolwork."

Dad feels relieved Eva is so willing to disclose her worries because, of course, it could easily be resolved. There is no urgency to doing the shopping, and he decides to go home and offer to help her attend to her homework.

"I think you may have gone shopping to avoid the work that was hard for you, but it caught up with you anyway. Maybe deep inside you even feared a panic attack about the math. Is that possible?"

"Now that you mention it, I think that could really be true. Sometimes in class when I know I don't understand the word problems, I start to get nervous and worry that I'll have a panic attack right there in school. I don't, but I do sometimes at home."

"So, let's go home, and we can look at the math problems together and set your mind at ease for the rest of the weekend."

They follow through on this plan but learn something essential: Eva tends to avoid something if she fears a panic attack. Avoidance isn't a good tactic compared to discussing her worry and working out a strategy to solve the problem she is apprehensive about. She and Dad agree that the next time she feels the need to avoid something, she will tell him, and they can make a plan together to take the edge off her anxiety.

TIPS FOR PARENTS OF CHILDREN WHO HAVE PANIC ATTACKS

1. With a panic attack, stepping back using Parental Intelligence is helpful because you don't lunge forward with a solution because the attack is often unexpected, and you don't understand it yet. But the parent needs to attend to the child's distress right away to relieve the attack as soon as possible.

2. In the story, Dad knew how to slow the attack and bring it to a halt with his plan to balance the oxygen and carbon dioxide by covering both

nose and mouth and breathing slowly. This can be done by cupping your hands over those areas on your face or using a paper bag (if it's available) to cover the child's nose and mouth.

3. Speaking slowly and comfortingly to the child and reminding them that the attack will wane and eventually stop is very relieving because it is common for a child in the middle of an attack to think it will go on forever, which increases anxiety.

4. Further, removing the child from the immediate environment of the attack is also relieving because that place could become linked with anxiety attacks in the future. So, when Dad took Eva out of the store, it was a wise maneuver.

5. Once the attack is over and the child is calm, it's helpful to learn about what's going on in her mind to find out if there was a trigger. Sometimes, when replaying the situation before the panic, the trigger is obvious, though often the trigger is internal (as was the case with Eva in the store) rather than external.

6. Finally, once the trigger is discovered, parent and child can collaborate and make a plan to solve the underlying problem.

As noted above, the prevalence of panic attacks is low in children, but some "gender differentiation is already observable in adolescence before the age fourteen years." Then the rates of panic disorders show a "gradual increase, particularly in girls, and possibly following the onset of puberty, and then peak during adulthood" (*Diagnostic Statistical Manual, Fifth Edition*, 210). Take, for example, Lara, age sixteen.

Lara is a cheerful, outgoing high performer in academics and athletics. President of her class, editor of the yearbook, and captain of the soccer team, she is headed for a high-ranking college. She studies and practices hard, but admittedly, these activities come rather easily for her. Her perseverance in adhering to a rigorous study and workout routine keeps her on top of her game in all respects. A junior in high school, she is already visiting colleges and hoping to play soccer in college. However, it seems that all of these achievements are made difficult not by her lack of talents, but by her anxiety. Like her mother, she is prone to anxiety attacks. Also, although not a consistent risk factor, when she was younger, she had significant separation anxiety (see Chapter 5).

Lara's anxiety attacks do not come out of the blue like Eva's in the grocery store. They usually precede high-pressure events like major exams, high-intensity soccer games, and award dinners. She has done her absolute best throughout the years not to avoid any of these events because they are important to her for her future and a major source of her high self-esteem. She learned these were the triggers after repeated panic attacks on the days of these events and asked her parents if she could go to psychotherapy to resolve the problem.

Lara, of course, is unusual in her proactive approach to her problem. She has high standards and goals for herself and, consistent with her approach to life, she wants to master her anxiety as well. The therapist referred her to a psychopharmacologist, who gave her Lexapro, a selective serotonin reuptake inhibitor (SSRI) that stops the panic attacks and moderates her general anxiety as well. Through talk therapy and engaging in many discussions with both her parents, she learns what sets off her attacks.

Following a panic attack at home that preceded the state championship soccer game, Mother and Lara agree they will have a talk the day after the game to get a grip on the triggers for these attacks. Mother hopes an open discussion will allow her to practice step three of Parental Intelligence, *understanding your child's mind.*

"Lara, it's a nice quiet Sunday. How about we talk about your panic attack yesterday? I'm glad you got a handle on it and the game went really great.

Congratulations for being the captain of a state champion soccer team!"

"Thanks. Yeah, I'm really ecstatic about the results. But, yes, I do need to understand my triggers. My therapist and I are working on it, but even the Lexapro didn't halt the attack completely, though it definitely made it shorter and I was able to gain control pretty quickly. Thank goodness for that."

"So, take your time and think of what kinds of thoughts and anticipations went through your mind, maybe during the week, and then peaked on Saturday morning before the game."

"Well, it's kind of hard to talk to you about this, and I admit I've been avoiding speaking to you even though my therapist urged me to if I wanted to share this. But to get to the point, deep down, I'm afraid to disappoint you and Daddy. I know the pressure comes from within me, but truthfully you and Daddy have always had high expectations for me. For a long time, you have complimented me on my talents, and though I know you think that praise is a good thing, it's also a pressure and stressor for me."

"Well, that is a big thing to come out with. I can see why you were reluctant to tell me that you and your therapist came to this discovery. I have to admit that Daddy and I do set the bar kind of high for you, knowing how gifted you are. We met in a top Ivy League school and hoped you'd be our legacy. It really wasn't fair to you, now that you are so clear about it. You should go to whatever college feels right for you, not for us. That's a big revelation for me to say, but I know it's the right one."

"I appreciate that you can admit to that, and I hope Daddy agrees because I don't want to go to your college. I want it to be my college. I want to leave my options open. I do want to go to a prestigious school, but the environment of the school matters a lot to me. I also want to feel like I'll fit in with the kids that attend the school and want to be pre-med. So, my needs really do have to come first. Does that make sense to you?"

"Yes, dear. This is so important. I'm so impressed with your honesty. It's okay to confront me. I need to hear this. But how does that fit in with the panic attacks?"

"Well, before any big events that measure my performance, I have in the back of my mind pleasing you and Dad. I'm trying to just please myself, but this is a new kind of understanding for me that my therapist has helped me with. The attack is related to a fear of disappointing you in the short and long run. Like, what if we didn't win yesterday? Truthfully, wouldn't you have been disappointed in me as captain of a losing team?"

The questions bring Mother back to step two of Parental Intelligence, *self-reflecting.* "I am trying to be truthful. I never succeeded like you have, even though

I went to a high-ranking college. You are exceptional, and I guess that gives me a kind of 'high' feeling. So, to answer your question, I might have been disappointed and told myself it was for you after all your work, but maybe deep inside I'm having you fulfill my wishes to be a great mother. That's wrong of me. You are your own person. You always have been, and I need to separate from you more and let you feel more autonomous. We've been so close, and even the idea of your going away to college is hard for me. I'll miss you so much. But I really have no excuses for letting my feelings affect you so much. I don't want to pressure you; you pressure yourself more than enough. You do have to find a school that's right for you. You're right. The quality of the environment and the peers you feel comfortable with matter a great deal. Forgive me, sweetheart, for overstepping."

"I think you are a great mother. How many mothers would be so honest and loving? You don't know how relieved I am to hear you say all that!"

"Really, you can't disappoint me, and I'm sure Daddy would agree. You need to talk to him too. We both do. Let's keep this talk going throughout the rest of the year. If you feel I do something to pressure you even in the most subtle of ways, don't hesitate to tell me. Gosh, I love you so much."

TIPS FOR PARENTS OF TEENS WHO HAVE PANIC ATTACKS

1. Listen attentively to your teens. Don't interrupt them before you truly understand what's on their minds.

2. Don't give advice or offer solutions because teens need to feel independent and know their vantage points are heard.

3. Recognize your teen's need for affirmation based on what is important to them. Their needs, desires, imaginings, and intentions need to be honored.

4. If Parental Intelligence is part of family life, teens will be able to disclose what's on their minds without fears of intimidation and rebuttal. They need to feel and know that their parents are not judging their opinions, but rather respecting them.

5. Not only teens, but also parents go through developmental stages. Adolescence in your kids is a developmental stage for you as parents. If your adolescence was rocky or pressured, you may need to resolve those old struggles if you are to really hear your teenager's struggles for what they are.

6. Encourage your teen's autonomy and independence.

7. It is helpful for parents to educate themselves about panic attacks. Google is a fine source for learning about them. Then they will be prepared to help their teen and also know when professional intervention is needed. Generally, recurrent attacks indicate that seeking psychotherapy is warranted.

8. The bottom line is always that mutual trust needs to be evident between parent and teen. Love needs to be coupled with honest communication, respect for each other's vantage points, and recurrent discussions of your teen's needs and wants as they discover themselves and establish their identity in the process of moving from early to middle to late adolescence.

HOW DO PARENTS KNOW IF PANIC ATTACKS ARE NORMAL OR ABNORMAL?

Generally, a panic attack is not normal; true attacks are indicators of severe anxiety. However, if your child or teen has a few isolated incidents of anxiety triggered by environmental stressors, but they don't resurface, there is no reason to be alarmed. It suggests the tendency is there, but if the attack is brief in duration and the child or teen tolerates the anxiety well, the likelihood of continuous panic attacks is not necessarily expected. Compassion is warranted, of course, but not undue worry or hasty action. However, keep in mind that predisposition to anxiety, and be alert for any further symptoms that do result in increased distress for your child or teen.

CHAPTER FOUR

OBSESSIVE-COMPULSIVE DISORDER

*E*ight-year-old Ward is a smart, good-looking boy, a bit short for his age, but a rapid learner, great chess player, and trampoline expert. The bane of his otherwise agreeable existence is his obsessive-compulsive disorder (OCD). Eight may seem young to develop OCD, but according to the *Diagnostic and Statistical Manual of Mental Disorders, Fifth Edition,* "nearly 25 percent of boys have an onset before ten years old," earlier than girls at that stage of development (239).

Toward the end of his seventh year, he showed signs of becoming a picky eater in that he had to have each food kept clearly separated on his plate or he was upset. Now, he has added to his observable compulsions in that he never eats leftovers and inspects the expiration date of any food offered him. He is afraid of germs. Furthermore, he has unexpected intrusive, aggressive thoughts of hurting his friends and parents, even though he is quite gentle and mild-mannered. While it is not always the case that kids with OCD have aggressive thoughts and this shouldn't be expected generally of all children with OCD, Ward is beset by such troubling thought patterns. He constantly worries about harm to himself and others, though he has never experienced either. Other compulsions that wax and wane are the need to wash his hands immediately after having aggressive thoughts and the need to check two or three times to make sure he turned the water off. These compulsions temporarily relieve his anxiety, but the thoughts do return later, resulting in a recurring pattern. An intrusive thought means it comes out of the blue without warning, which is very distressing because the child doesn't feel in control of his mind.

The compulsion is the mind's way of trying to undo the troubling thought, but this mechanism fails although it occurs repeatedly.

Ward's father is a stay-at-home dad. His mother is a doctor, away each day for a good eight hours. Both parents are beside themselves trying to live around Ward's desperate needs. They wisely sought assistance from a therapist who advised them to not be angry with Ward for his compulsions because this was an illness, not willful acts that discipline could eliminate. The parents are loath to give such a young child medication, so they hope that psychotherapy will alleviate most of his symptoms.

Following the steps of Parental Intelligence, Ward's parents step back when they see a compulsion so as not to raise Ward's anxiety further. They know they feel sad, scared, and sometimes annoyed that these compulsions interfere with Ward's general functioning at home, and they kind of tiptoe around him when they are together.

At school, however, the OCD does not seem to be a problem—except at lunchtime. If Ward buys his food at school, other kids see him separate his food items on his plate. Though the other children don't fuss about it because Ward is such a likable guy, Ward is self-conscious, so he brings sandwiches and bags of treats from home to avoid the problem.

The therapist advised the parents to be open with Ward about his OCD but not to pressure him to stop his compulsions as that might only exacerbate the problem. They let him separate his foods, as long as he eats a balanced diet and keeps his weight up, which isn't difficult. He is a very good eater actually, and doesn't refuse any foods at all. They don't emphasize expiration dates and they don't comment when Ward checks them. Now and then, they reassure Ward that germs are not a problem in their house, but otherwise, they let Ward act on his compulsions without interference or judgment.

While Ward's parents' efforts do address his outward symptoms, they are unaware of the aggressive thoughts he faces each day. Because Ward had always kept his aggressive thoughts to himself, his parents had no idea he was facing those thoughts and feelings alone. Not all children with OCD experience intrusive aggressive thoughts, so they didn't know about them until Ward asked his therapist to share them with his parents. The therapist waited for this permission, not wanting to betray Ward's trust in her before then. Confidentiality was very important to Ward and, of course, to his therapist. Eventually, with the support from his therapist, Ward shared those aggressive thoughts with his parents on his own as well. As his parents think back on the previous months, they realize that there might have been indicators of inner turmoil. Both parents had noticed that Ward tended to apologize too quickly and very profusely if he bumped into someone or if he felt angry and shoved his brother ever so lightly. These extra apologies tipped them off that something was bothering Ward, but it wasn't until Ward and his therapist explained that he often had thoughts of really hurting people—and subsequently felt extremely guilty—that the apologies made sense. After a year of once-a-week psychotherapy, the apologies stopped.

Both at home and in therapy, Ward draws pictures of angry people hurting each other with guns, which, to the unknowing observer, would just look like any kid's drawings of superheroes or good and bad guys. For Ward, however, he is playing out his thoughts, which help him a great deal. He and the therapist discuss his feelings about being *nice* and *mean*, typical words for a boy his age, and how everyone makes mistakes and has angry thoughts now and then.

Furthermore, the therapist advises the parents to speak easily and openly about their random annoyances at each other, giving words to their feelings. If they are frustrated with something they are doing, they should vocalize that frustration to demonstrate to Ward that such emotions and feelings are commonplace, even though they aren't sweet and nice. The therapist emphasizes that thoughts and deeds are different. Being angry at someone doesn't mean you actually hurt that person; thoughts and actions were distinct.

As Ward's intrusive thoughts lessen and he becomes aware that experiencing a range of feelings is natural and normal, the need for his compulsions lessens and he stops washing his hands and checking the water faucet to make sure it was turned off. In time, as his aggressive thoughts become more normalized (*"It's okay to be mad at your father"*), his fear of germs also lessens and he slowly begins to eat more easily, letting foods touch each other. His father assists at first with the expiration dates by telling Ward to check just once, not several times, and eventually, as the intrusive thoughts lessen, Ward forgets about the expiration dates altogether.

This is a success story, generally speaking, because the parents have an understanding therapist who guides them well and because they use empathy, not punishment or yelling, in keeping with their belief in the Parental Intelligence approach. They also expanded Ward's social life, increasing the frequency of his play dates, having him attend a chess club with boys his age, and joining a gym for kids with trampolines. Socializing in these ways enlarged his world, which is developmentally appropriate for an eight-year-old, and further diverted his attention from his inner world to the larger world outside of him.

TIPS FOR PARENTS OF CHILDREN WITH OCD

1. Early intervention is essential. When parents notice the first signs of compulsions—which they will see because they are observable (unlike obsessive thoughts, which are hidden)—getting professional help right away prevents the OCD from becoming chronic and fixed.

2. Monitor your own reactions by self-reflecting on how your child's behavior makes you feel. If you skip this step of Parental Intelligence, you may find yourself yelling at the child for his actions, which would only increase the anxiety and consequently worsen the compulsions.

3. Reassure the child about the distinctions between pretend and real, and between thoughts and actions. This helps him see that, for example, the germs are a fear in his mind, not threatening in reality.

4. Recognize that OCD is a disease. This will help you avoid becoming punitive if you become annoyed by the inconveniences the disorder causes. There's a great tendency for adults to just tell a child to stop their compulsions, to use willpower and self-discipline. This fails and, in fact, exacerbates the anxiety, which

in turn increases the OCD and furthermore makes the child feel that he isn't understood and then he feels alone with his plight. Feeling alone makes a child feel crazy, scared, and filled with self-doubts, which again only increases the anxiety.

5. Parents need to help and support each other. As you share your fears with each other and utilize the guidance of a therapist, it can help alleviate your painful worries about your child. Parents need to feel like a team with the therapist in caring for their anxious child. Single parents can find comfort in sharing their thoughts with a close friend or professional. This can help relieve excessive worry and sort out the best ways to guide their children.

When Ward turned seventeen, the developmental pressures of adolescence stirred his OCD again. His compulsions now are more about ordering his books and papers in specific ways, making sure his homework is perfectly neat (or he'd throw it away and start again), and filling in the little circles on standardized tests—also perfectly, which of course slowed him down. His aggressive thoughts returned, and now, as a stronger male adolescent, he expresses his urges in a disciplined way through athletics, but this doesn't erase his thinking process. He begins hand washing again, and this time it is worse, his hands becoming red and sore.

At this time, the parents return to the same therapist, and she recommends a medication evaluation by a psychopharmacologist who works with teenagers. Ward is given both medication to reduce anxiety (Clonazapam) and an SSRI (Fluvoxamine). An SSRI is a selective serotonin reuptake inhibitor, an anti-depressant that is also used for OCD. This means the serotonin, a chemical that sends signals between nerve cells, is inhibited or held in the brain longer to be more effective. The Fluvoxamine is later changed to Paroxatine, which is more effective for Ward. Sometimes more than one SSRI must be tried to meet the individual chemistry of the patient.

The combination of psychotherapy and medication once again relieves Ward, and he can adjust to his compulsions, attend college and post-graduate school quite successfully, and lead a productive life in later years. The psychotherapy is even more effective for teens because their ability for abstract thinking, and thus insight into their thoughts and feelings, is enhanced.

TIPS FOR PARENTS OF TEENS WITH OCD

1. While the onset for OCD may come in childhood or adolescence, the Parental Intelligence approach is applicable at any age, along with (as early as possible) professional intervention.

2. Once again, it's essential to treat your teen with respect and not make him feel odd or crazy. OCD is a very painful emotional mental state that requires compassion and support.

3. Expect that medication doesn't always work quickly or easily for many teens and that months may go by before finding which medication works best. Helping your teen tolerate this waiting period is a difficult task for parents who are also impatient for their child to feel relief.

4. Because OCD can slow a teen down and make schoolwork a trial, don't be afraid to assist your teen with projects or college applications by typing in the essential data and editing essays. This is not doing the work for the teen or undermining his autonomy; it is recognizing the limitations the OCD puts on him as he is pressured to complete multiple assignments or applications.

5. Encourage your teen to socialize, despite his emotional duress. Socialization is essential to his developmental progress, and teens these days are generally very tolerant of other kids with emotional struggles. Lots of kids take various medications, and while you, the parent, may want to keep the condition private, don't be surprised if your teen confides in a few close friends.

6. As always, a close and trusting parent-teen relationship is the best support for OCD. When your teen knows you are his ally and are doing your best to understand his duress, there is minimal rebellion and independence can be respected.

7. Remember that OCD is not your teen's whole life. Be open to his opinions and viewpoints about all kinds of subjects so he feels respected by you and can build his self-esteem.

HOW DO PARENTS KNOW IF SYMPTOMS OF OCD ARE NORMAL OR ABNORMAL?

Children and teens establish routines in their daily lives that keep them organized. This is healthy and expected. In fact, from a young age, parents encourage routines.

Routines surrounding bedtime, hygiene, homework, and chores are just a few examples. Some children and teens stick very closely to them, so they become daily rituals that keep life orderly and consistent, making room for increasingly complex lives. It is only worrisome if the child loses some flexibility when it's called for and worries excessively if their routines vary somewhat.

Some kids do have more or less obsessive personalities without having an obsessive-compulsive disorder. Many children and teens worry unnecessarily at times when something seems of extra importance to them. When the event or stressor passes, the worry ceases. It's wise for parents to keep an eye on this obsessing, but not to be alarmed. If there are no compulsions that coincide with the obsessions and if the worry passes with the stressor, OCD is not diagnosed.

On the other hand, if you notice your child is unusually worried, tense, and preoccupied with his thoughts and, in addition, you observe specific compulsions to ward off these thoughts, you should recognize these are signs of OCD. It may become apparent that these symptoms are interfering with your teen's general functioning at home and at school. Early intervention before the obsessions and compulsions become too habituated is clearly advisable. Remember to exercise compassion and empathy with Parental Intelligence. Mothers and fathers who routinely use the steps of Parental Intelligence have created a trusted bond with their teen, so that they can gently approach him about their observations and offer to help the adolescent relieve himself of his emotional duress. The teen will feel loved and cared for and deeply appreciative of his parents' involvement with what has been plaguing him secretly. Once again, the parent-teen bond will be strengthened as the adolescent feels protected and more secure with his parents' love and support.

CHAPTER FIVE

SEPARATION ANXIETY

*C*ici is a delightful, generally cheerful eight-year-old with long hair that reaches her waist; she takes pride in that. She is an only child with two working parents. Her parents have always provided excellent child care for her from the time she was six months old: first at home and then, when she turned three, at a small day care setting in the home of a certified child minder for her age group.

There were only five children in the home day care, so Cici received a great deal of attention and got along well with the other kids. Despite the positive situation, Cici's transition to this home was a difficult one. This was not unexpected because she was very attached to her parents and the original caretaker. But at three years old, children often need reassurances that they will see their parents at the end of the day.

What exacerbated Cici's situation was that her parents worked long hours, and because she went to sleep fairly early, the time she spent with them in the evenings was limited. To alleviate what was then seen as normal anxiety for a three-year-old under these circumstances, the original caretaker planned to greet Cici after she left the child-minder's home after the five-hour day there. Shortening the time with the child-minder to five hours and seeing her caretaker complicated the situation in some respects, but it set Cici's mind at ease—as well as her parents'. The caretaker stayed with her from two o'clock to five, when her mother came home.

Life seemed to move along well for Cici as she progressed in age, entering kindergarten at five years old and again getting along nicely with her peers and responding to the authority of the nurturing teacher in a healthy way: following the classroom routines, sharing easily with the other children, and learning the academic requirements of that beginning grade.

Now Cici is almost eight years old, and her parents are concerned, and even a little annoyed, that she still wants to sleep in their bed for the first part of the night before she can settle down and return to her own room.

Her parents have always felt a bit guilty for working so much, although their careers were very important to them, so they had never insisted that she sleep entirely in her own bed. In fact, they like the cuddling at night as well because they miss their little girl during the day. However, Cici's parents finally face the fact that not being able to sleep alone from the start of bedtime was beyond normal expectations for a third grader.

Two months prior to her eighth birthday, they have a gentle talk with Cici. They set a goal that by her birthday, she will be sleeping in her own bed in her own room throughout the night. Cici protests at first, but somehow she knows that she is different from her peers in this respect, and deep inside she does wish for the independence of her own space at night.

Her parents proceed slowly, creating a new routine for Cici to be read to in her own bed, use a night light, and start to get in her own bed at 7:30 in the evening. For half an hour, the parents read and chat and settle her down in a calm way. At first, after turning out the room lights, Cici begs to get in her parents' bed. They consistently say "No" to this request, but one of them sits by her side while she falls asleep in her own bed. Incrementally, they remove themselves further by sitting in a chair in her room while she falls asleep instead of on her bed. Again, she protests, but slowly adapts. When her birthday comes, she has successfully tolerated her parents leaving her in her room without sitting in the chair—or so it seemed at first.

Then after about two days of this success, she starts coming to their room during the night and slipping under the covers next to her mother. She is quiet, and the parents are deep sleepers, so it takes an hour or so for them to notice she is there. Cici's mother walks the half-asleep Cici back to bed where she sleeps the rest of the night in her bed.

This continues, however, for a month before the parents have another discussion with her about staying in her bed the whole night. She confesses to being afraid of the dark, missing her parents, and fearing a kidnapper would take her away and she'd never see her parents again.

Separation anxiety is now clearly evident and has progressed to some reluctance to go to school. Cici dawdles in the morning, delaying getting dressed and eating her breakfast so she is always rushing to the bus.

Using Parental Intelligence, the parents step back and do their best to hide their annoyance as they, too, are busy people getting prepared for their day at work. They each reflect on their mounting annoyance and worry about the possibility of things getting worse. When Cici protests one evening that her parents are going out to dinner without her, they finally had to face that her separation anxiety was real and significant.

Using step three of Parental Intelligence, "Understanding Your Child's Mind," they sit down together one quiet Saturday morning to discuss the problem. Cici tries to avoid the discussion by dancing around and making jokes, but she realizes quickly enough that her parents are serious. They use the term "separation anxiety" to explain to her that she is becoming excessively worried about their leaving her for periods of time. Silently, they fear she will develop a school phobia as well.

Cici is used to talking openly with her parents and emphasizes in clear and direct terms that she misses her parents terribly during the day, and although she loves her caretaker, she can barely wait until five o'clock for her mother to arrive home. She is sometimes scared that her mother won't ever return, that something terrible has happened to her, and then she'd only have her father, who she also fears might be harmed.

Her parents explain the difference between fear and anxiety. Her mother says, "Being afraid of something real, like a bear at the front door, is totally reasonable. But Mommy and Daddy are always on time, and nothing bad has ever happened in your whole life to make you suspect that we wouldn't come home! Your fears about our well-being when we're separated is something only younger kids worry about, so we're going to help you with this because it's not realistic actually."

Still, Cici's parents understand that her fears feel very real to her. To ease the burden Cici was experiencing, they decide together that her mother would call her or text her at four o'clock each day to reassure her she was coming home in an hour. Cici likes this plan very much. It eases her anxiety tremendously, and in time, she no longer fears she would be left alone, insecure and frightened. She even tells them that they don't need to call or text her each day because it interrupts what she is doing.

Because the parents collaborated with Cici after listening carefully to her fears, they are on the right track. Furthermore, they increase her involvement with her peers after school so Cici is distracted and more engaged with girls her age, normal for her development at this point.

Cici even joins some after-school activities. She especially enjoys an arts and crafts group at a local art center the caretaker brings her to, and by the time she is eight-and-a-half years old, the problems are resolved. It was a long and gradual road, but her anxiety diminished appreciably and she is now more engaged with her peers and continues to do well at school. Her development is finally on track.

TIPS FOR PARENTS OF CHILDREN WITH SEPARATION ANXIETY

1. Watch for early signs. Recurring excessive distress in anticipation of separation from major attachment figures needs to be recognized as early as possible by the age of three. Prior to that, it is to be expected that kids need to learn that when parents go away, they come back.

2. Establish bedtime routines from infancy on. This creates a secure atmosphere for separating from parents gradually as children age.

3. Especially in dual-working households or single-parent working households, it is to be expected that children will react eventually to the absence of their parents, especially when there is a change from the primary substitute caretaking experience. During such transitions, set clear expectations for your child so she feels secure and safe with new attachment figures.

4. It is helpful for working parents to have contact with their children during the day before entering kindergarten. A once-a-day call to the caretaker can be quite reassuring to the parent that things are going well. If needed, your child can get on the phone for a quick "hello," telling you what she's been doing.

5. When you return from work, it's important to leave your career at the door and attend to your child, who has missed you during the day. Giving your full attention to your child—without phone calls or other distractions—with a comfortable evening meal, alleviates the stressors of the day.

6. As mentioned in previous chapters, the reliable relationship and bond between parents and child is crucial to solve separation issues. The child internalizes a deep trust in her parents that helps her problem solve when anxieties recur. The relationship is key.

Carl just turned eighteen and is looking forward to attending college away from home in the fall. He worked hard during high school to get good grades and spent time on extracurricular activities to build a résumé that would help him receive an acceptance to the school of his choice. As most high school seniors do, Carl worried he would be rejected from all the schools he applied to, but he was glad to receive more acceptances than rejections and settled on a school to his liking. He wants to be an architect and is anticipating a rigorous five-year program at a university about a six-hour drive from home.

Carl had a great experience away from home after his junior year attending a summer program traveling for five weeks with his peers to different sites to see modern architecture being built around the country. This was an unusual program his parents found, and he was so excited to be enrolled. This required living in hotels for six weeks with peers he didn't know. He got along well with a diverse group of kids, and while he kept in contact with his parents several times a week, he seemed to fare well in being away from home.

However, during July before going away from college, he begins to experience separation anxiety. He knows this will not be a five-week stint but a more permanent away-from-home arrangement. He has always been close to his parents and relies on their good advice and support. He feels fairly independent with his friends and school activities, bolstered by his travel, but he notices increasing anxiety as the summer progresses. He has a job working at a construction site, which is great preparation for his future academic work and anticipated career, and while working he feels fine. But in the evenings, when he and his mother shop for needed supplies to live away from home, he feels reluctant and worried.

His mother notices he is procrastinating shopping with her for the needed clothes and dorm room materials like bedding, towels, and such, and wonders why. Furthermore, he finds odd reasons to avoid his physical at the doctor required by the school and puts off going on social media to find a roommate. She finds it somewhat frustrating that he isn't getting things done in an organized way, so he can be prepared for college.

After stepping back to see if he would handle things himself and self-reflecting on her own frustration and worry, she sits with Carl and points out the pattern of his procrastination.

"Carl, this isn't like you. What is on your mind about going away to college?"

Carl hemmed and hawed but eventually said, "I'm worried about living so far away. I feel like I will barely see you and Dad, and I'll miss you terribly."

His mother reminds him that parents' visiting day was in October, just a month after school started, but that doesn't ease his mind. He also worries that he won't make friends easily, even though he had on his trip the summer before.

His mother remembers his early separation anxiety experiences when he entered middle school. The transition from elementary school was hard for him as he suddenly was faced with multiple teachers, increased schoolwork, and peers from various elementary schools coming together. They worked through it at the time, but it took about two months for him to settle down. Like now, he seemed to become anxious about being away from home.

She reminds him of that transition, and they discuss how he had a tendency for separation anxiety when he was making a school change. Together they recall how he coped successfully by allowing himself to make a slow transition and not expecting to be immediately settled when he was away from home.

"We can follow that same pattern this fall," his mother said. "We can talk to each other every day at first, until you feel more settled."

Carl is reassured. Actually, just talking about it makes Carl feel less alone, and his procrastination stops. He even finds a roommate.

For Carl, expressing his fears and feeling understood was mostly what solved the problem, relieving his anxiety. Keeping his worries to himself had only increased and exaggerated them.

TIPS FOR PARENTS OF TEENS WITH SEPARATION ANXIETY

1. Don't overact to early signs of separation anxiety. Use Parental Intelligence to step back before you act.

2. When you begin to get anxious that your teen is showing symptoms, use that anxiety as a clue to your teenager's anxiety. In other words, when you feel anxious, you may be sensing what your teen might be feeling. This will help you empathize with him.

3. Plan summer activities away from home prior to your teen's senior year to help him gradually grow accustomed to being away from home.

4. Remind your teen of his successes away from home in making new friends, especially if this is a potential worry.

5. Face separation anxiety clearly with your teen to help him confront the problem and see what is *excessive* worry compared to what is realistic and can be planned for.

6. If your teen has experienced separation problems earlier in life, be on alert that there may be a regression when the teen reaches a new developmental phase or transition in his life.

HOW DO PARENTS KNOW IF SYMPTOMS OF SEPARATION ANXIETY ARE NORMAL OR ABNORMAL?

Up to age three, parents should consider that separation anxiety may be following a normal developmental course. Beyond that, kids should feel fairly confident that their parents will return after being away for a period of time. As we have seen in these examples, some children have difficulty with transitions from one developmental stage to another. This is when the tendency for separation anxiety perks up.

Prolonged separation anxiety is an abnormal mental state for teens generally speaking, but it may be triggered by new challenges away from home as we saw with Carl. Using Parental Intelligence to collaboratively problem solve the distress after listening attentively to your child's fears and worries helps a great deal. The base of separation anxiety is a fear of being alone and insecure. Sharing those concerns with an attentive, nonjudgmental, listening parent offers teens a great deal of relief. Then the teen feels less alone and can cope with what becomes a normal amount of anxiety when facing significant changes.

RESOLVING THE PARENT-CHILD ANXIETY SPIRAL AND ENJOYING LIFE

*A*pprehensive uneasiness or nervousness, often over an impending or anticipated experience, is common for children and teens with or without chronic anxiety. We have seen the wide variations in the manifestations of anxiety in children and teens that you, the busy parent, can help modify and often remedy with

Parental Intelligence. It is a continuous process to build an alliance between you and your child or teen, and this will deepen your relationship. When you are careful to not judge your anxious child or teen or blame her for her plight, you become an ally and she doesn't feel alone. Even when you are not actually there, the child has internalized that bond and will feel your supportive alliance. It's important that you see the whole child; anxiety is just a part of her. When you have that perspective, your child feels accepted without a sense of shame.

As noted in the many examples in this book, anxiety can come at unexpected times, episodically for some and chronically for others. You have learned that anxiety is a multisystem response to a perceived threat. There are biochemical changes in the body, and your child or teen's personal history of anxiety has a bearing on her future experiences. In order to empathize fully with our children, it bears repeating that anxious children experience an abnormal and overwhelming sense of fear, often marked by physical autonomic signs such as tension, sweating, chest pain, panic, increased heart or pulse rate, trembling, gastrointestinal complaints, fatigue, trouble sleeping, and intrusive thoughts quelled by compulsions combined with doubt about the reality of the threat and self-doubt about one's capacity to tolerate or cope with it.

It is important to distinguish between anxiety as a feeling or experience and anxiety as a disorder with a psychiatric diagnosis. A child or teen may feel anxious without having an anxiety disorder as such. Moreover, a child or teen facing a clear and present danger with realistic fear is not usually considered to be in a mental state of anxiety.

Although anxiety is commonplace, in that everyone experiences anxious feelings from time to time, there are many different potential causes and degrees of intensity at different developmental stages in children and teens' lives. Using Parental Intelligence is a simple approach busy parents like you can take to determine and help your child or teen with any form of anxiety.

If parental guidance is not sufficient and you feel that the anxiety is abnormal, seek professional help. Anxiolytics or medications that help to relieve anxiety are also useful for some kids and teens.

As we have seen, anxiety can follow different courses. Anxiety that lacks a definite focus or content is called free-floating anxiety, usually symptomatic of generalized anxiety or overanxious disorder in childhood. Contrast that to more definitive forms of anxiety, such as a panic disorder, obsessive-compulsive disorder, and separation anxiety. Concomitant with any of these more specific forms of anxiety could be the development of a phobia, which is a psychological defense against anxiety where the child or teen displaces their anxious feelings onto an external object, activity, or situation.

We have also seen that although anxiety is related to fear, it is not the same, so we need to empathize differently and follow different courses of action. *Fear* is more clearly focused on a specific event or object that the person is consciously aware of, and it has a distinct cause, such as an actual intruder in the home or an out-of-control fire. In contrast, as the examples have demonstrated, *anxiety* is experienced as emotional pain and the child or teen may not immediately know the source of the feeling. While most people are fearful in physically dangerous situations and can agree that such fear is an appropriate response to danger, anxiety is generally triggered by objects and events specific to the individual child or teen. It is essential that we empathize with each child or teen's individual experience. While occasional anxiety is part of normal life, children and teens with anxiety disorders frequently have intense, excessive, persistent worry about everyday situations, sometimes peaking within minutes (panic attacks). These feelings can interfere with daily activities.

It is also important to address your anxiety as the parent, as well as that of your child or teen, which on the one hand can help you understand what your child or teen is going through, but on the other hand can exacerbate your youngster's anxious state of mind.

Parents suffer when their kids suffer. If your child or teen's anxiety raises your own, then a spiral can begin where each person's tension increases the other's. An anxious youngster needs a steady, stable parent to calm them down. This is done initially if the parent wisely uses the first step of Parental Intelligence, *stepping back*. By reacting slowly and with ease to your child's edginess, taking the time to pause and consider the situation before bursting in with fast solutions, your child will sense your pace and slowly internalize it. Eventually, we hope that the child can learn to control their own anxiety by slowing down their motor, so to speak, to understand what they are experiencing enough to take some steps to modify their restlessness and come to grips with the causes of their nervous state of mind with your help.

If the spiral begins, it doesn't mean all is lost. The parent can still *step back* midstream, *self-reflect*, and quickly consider what is prompting his or her own anxiety. When a parent is busy, this step is often left out, though in the long run, it saves time because self-understanding then leads to understanding your reactions to your child. Then you can *step back* once more and begin to *understand your child or teen's mind* while also *understanding his or her stage of development*, the next steps in Parental Intelligence. If the busy parent has internalized this process, it will come naturally with each new anxious episode, and the child will incorporate the process as well.

Anxiety, as we now know, consists of various physical autonomic reactions, beyond the person's control that can throw both you and your child or teen way off kilter. When busy parents learn these signs and symptoms well, they know how to intervene with their child effectively. Your child or teen at first relies upon your responses, but the ultimate goal is for the youngster to be able to gain control when you are absent.

Avoidance is a common reaction to the anticipation of anxiety, and children and teens go to great pains to avoid anxiety-causing situations. As we have seen, symptoms may start in early childhood and/or teen years, and they can continue into adulthood. This prevents anxious children or teens from realizing their potential in many areas of life and restricts their accomplishments and general self-confidence.

We want to help stretch our kids, not further their tendency to restrict themselves. When carrying out step three, *understanding your child's mind*, discuss with your child the mechanism of avoidance and how it's a detriment to enjoying life. Then with step five, *problem solving*, discuss and create alternative pathways for coping with anxiety that lead to resolving interpersonal and internal pain.

In my thirty years of treating parents, children, and teens with anxiety, I have found that even those with chronic anxiety can enjoy the pleasures of life and learn to love, work, and play, not only expanding their repertoire of coping mechanisms, but actually resolving their initial tendency to react nervously. They can learn how to move forward with confidence and heightened self-esteem.

It is abundantly clear that stable, supportive, secure, safe parent-child and parent-teen relationships are the most important key elements to resolving anxiety experiences. As a parent, your non-judgmental, empathic responses to anxiety help children and teens cope and resolve these highly tension-producing experiences. With a clear, consistent Parental Intelligence approach, even as a busy parent, you can lovingly meet your kids' needs for relief and, ultimately, resolution of different kinds of anxiety.

Anxiety is an internal challenge that, when examined and conquered, can lead to a sense of mastery and a deeper sense of one's self. With Parental Intelligence, professional guidance as needed, and sometimes medication, there is no reason for anxious youngsters to not lead fulfilling and gratifying lives. When it's understood that there is meaning behind anxiety underlying this state of mind, then both adults and children become *meaning-makers*—solving problems, furthering their interests and pursuits, and finding how to love and be loved.

REFERENCES

American Psychiatric Association. *Diagnostic and Statistical Manual of Mental Disorders*, 5th ed. Arlington, VA: American Psychiatric Association, 2013.

Hollman, Laurie. *Unlocking Parental Intelligence: Finding Meaning in Your Child's Behavior*. Sanger, California: Familius, 2015.

ABOUT THE AUTHOR

LAURIE HOLLMAN, PhD, is a psychoanalyst with specialized clinical training in infant-parent, child, adolescent, and adult psychotherapy covering the lifespan. She is the author of the Gold Mom's Choice Award book, *Unlocking Parental Intelligence: Finding Meaning in Your Child's Behavior* and *The Busy Parent's Guide to Managing Anger in Children and Teens: The Parental Intelligence Way.*

Dr. Hollman has been on the faculties of New York University, The Society for Psychoanalytic Study and Research (where she was president), Long Island University, and the Long Island Institute for Psychoanalysis.

She has written extensively for various publications on infant, child, and adolescent development, including the *Psychoanalytic Study of the Child*, *The International Journal of Infant Observation*, and *The Inner World of the Mother*. She has also written on subjects relevant to parents for the *Family Law Review*, a publication of the New York Bar Association. As a columnist for *Newday's Parents & Children Magazine* and the *Long Island Parent* for almost a decade, she has also written numerous articles on parenting.

Dr. Hollman wrote the "Parental Intelligence" column for *Moms Magazine*, blogs for *Huffington Post*, and writes for *Thrive Global*. She has also been a feature writer for *Pittsburgh Parent, The Bay State Parent Magazine*, and *Active Family Magazine* and a guest writer for popular parenting websites, including *The Bloggy Moms Network, Natural Parenting Network, Positive Parenting Ally, Our Parent Spot*, and *Parenting London Child*.

Dr. Hollman and her husband are the proud parents of two spirited, industrious, and loving sons.

ABOUT FAMILIUS

Visit Our Website: www.familius.com

Join Our Family

There are lots of ways to connect with us! Subscribe to our newsletters at www.familius.com to receive uplifting daily inspiration, essays from our Pater Familius, a free ebook every month, and the first word on special discounts and Familius news.

Get Bulk Discounts

If you feel a few friends and family might benefit from what you've read, let us know and we'll be happy to provide you with quantity discounts. Simply email us at orders@familius.com.

Connect

- Facebook: www.facebook.com/paterfamilius
- Twitter: @familiustalk, @paterfamilius1
- Pinterest: www.pinterest.com/familius
- Instagram: @familiustalk

The most important work you ever do will be within the walls of your own home.

CPSIA information can be obtained
at www.ICGtesting.com
Printed in the USA
FSHW01n1021180618
49434FS

9 781641 700108